Drawn by N. Whittock   *Heddon Church*   *Engraved by J. Shury*

DEATH COMES TO HEDON

The Cholera Epidemic of 1849

by

Margaret and Bob Cochrane

Highgate Publications (Beverley) Ltd
1993

British Library Cataloguing in Publication Data
Cochrane, Margaret Ruth
  Death Comes to Hedon: Cholera Epidemic of 1849
  I. Title   II. Cochrane, Robert Euan
  614.5140942838

ISBN 0-948929-80-4

ISBN 0 948929 80 4

Published by
Highgate Publications (Beverley) Ltd.
24 Wylies Road, Beverley, HU17 7AP
Telephone (0482) 866826

Produced by
B. A. Print
4 Newbegin, Lairgate, Beverley, HU17 8EG
Telephone (0482) 886017

Contents

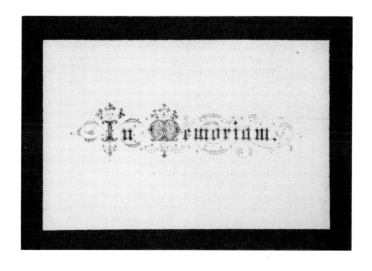

Preface

In 1977 I telephoned my brother David who lived in Perth to let him know we were moving to Hedon. I told him I did not expect he would know where that was. He surprised me immediately by saying, "Oh yes, that attractive little town, the other side of Hull, with the cobbled market and the large church with the blue clock." He further went on to surprise me by saying he had a history of Hedon which he had bought in a second-hand bookshop in Perth for a very modest sum.

He said he would let me have this and it turned out to be a copy of Boyle's *Early History of Hedon*. We found the details of our new home town fascinating and this led us to take an interest in Hedon's past.

We were even more enthralled to find tucked away between the leaves a very old typescript copy of a moving account of the Cholera Epidemic by Henry Brown, the churchwarden, taken from the minutes of the Hedon Parish Church Vestry Book. This account, which is printed in full at the end of our book, set us on the trail to find out more about what actually happened and eventually resulted in this book.

Bob Cochrane.
September 1993.

Epidemics in England

It is only in the last 150 years that improvements in hygiene and medicine have led to a vast reduction in infectious diseases. Into our own century, deaths from smallpox, typhus, diphtheria and tuberculosis have been common. Minor epidemics have come and gone but major epidemics which have had a serious effect on the country as a whole have been rare.

The arrival in England of the Black Death in 1384 was one such occasion. After sweeping its way from central Asia across Europe in the preceding year it must have seemed like a visitation from God to the afflicted population. They did not know that it was spread by the bites of fleas living on the brown rats which had recently migrated to Europe from the East. They did not know that the disease could also be caught by breathing the droplets exhaled when an infected person sneezed or coughed. They did know that if they caught the disease they were unlikely to survive. In 1348 between a quarter and a third of the population died. Whole villages were deserted and cultivated land reverted to its natural state. Truly this epidemic deserved its name, the Black Death.

The next major outbreak was in 1665 — The Great Plague of London, although not confined to that city. This again was the Bubonic Plague, which left the following year. After this there was a long gap until the 19th century before the next major sickness to reach plague proportions — Cholera.

Cholera Strikes

Asiatic cholera had been endemic in Bengal for many years and soldiers and officials of the East India Company would be well aware of its depredations. However, it was unknown in Great Britain before the first third of the 19th century. With the movement of pilgrims visiting the Ganges, and soldiers, both native and British, travelling to and from the Company's headquarters at Calcutta, outbreaks spread throughout the subcontinent from time to time.

Whether there was some mutation in the cholera germ, or whether it was just a quirk of fate, following a particularly violent outbreak in 1817, cholera started on its peregrinations, first travelling north-east and ravaging China, and then gradually spreading over south-east Asia and the islands of Indonesia.

Movement north-west was slower but cholera crept inexorably over Afghanistan, Persia, southern Russia, and westward across Europe. Although the progress of the disease could be seen, any efforts to stop it appeared useless. The epidemic reached the Baltic in 1831, whence some unfortunate seaman or traveller carried it to Britain. The first recorded case in Britain was in Sunderland on 26 October 1831. The disease spread rapidly in all directions, reaching London and Edinburgh in February 1832, and Dublin a month later.

Local health committees were set up but these were amateurs with no particular knowledge, a multitude of theories and treatments and no authority or funds to act. The Privy Council appointed a general fast but, being no respecter of persons, the disease took its course.

This first epidemic gradually subsided but, on hearing from the Continent of further outbreaks there, the Government appointed a Central Board of Health in 1848 — exactly one week before cholera struck again. The epidemic raged throughout late 1848 and into 1849. It was this epidemic which hit Hedon in the summer of the latter year.

The Nature of Cholera

The speed with which it killed and the shrunken appearance of its victims made this a particularly terrifying disease. One could never feel safe with cholera around, knowing that from fitness to death might only be a matter of a few hours. The symptoms, severe diarrhoea of a watery nature and sudden violent vomiting, quickly dehydrate the body. The victim becomes wizened, with features shrunken, eyes depressed. The blood thickens and causes discolouring to the skin like bruising. This is accompanied by a high fever and sometimes cramps and spasms of the arms and legs. After a few hours the patient becomes very weak and feeble, the pulse rate drops and becomes barely detectable, and death may follow. In other cases the patient lingers on in this state for some time before recovering or expiring.

Although this was less than 150 years ago, the medicine of the time was in a primitive state. Doctors were still arguing over the causes of disease. Some inclined to the "atmospheric" or "miasmatic" theory. This assumed that the disease was spread by a gas or bad air given off by rotting materials. The "germ" theory of disease had been around for many years but no one had been able to prove the existence of germs. During the Napoleonic wars, a French army of 30,000 men had been sent to the

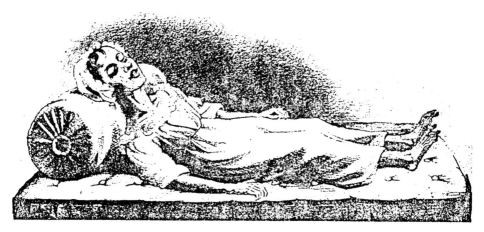

The wizened appearance of a cholera victim.

West Indies and had been decimated by yellow fever. As they had not been in contact with the disease, this was considered to disprove the germ theory and support the miasmatic theory which was in the ascendent in the first half of the 19th century. Therefore, doctors took no steps to trace the germ, and such medical treatment as was given was usually of an experimental nature and often worse than the disease. The main treatment for cholera seemed to be Calomel and Laudanum, sometimes little and often, sometimes massive doses; but emetics, bleeding and various substances which we would now class as poison were all used. One doctor reported success in rehydrating patients with saline solution, which is a modern and effective method, but his reports were discredited by other doctors. It was not until later in the century that real progress was made.

Following the 1849 epidemic Dr. John Snow put forward the theory that cholera was caused by polluted drinking water, and not inhaled as generally believed. He was an early believer in anaesthesia, and had administered chloroform to Queen Victoria to help in childbirth. In spite of his connections he was considered something of a crank with his new-fangled ideas, and, whilst his theory had its backers, general medical opinion thought it nonsense.

However, in the epidemic of 1853 he plotted the cases occurring around Broad Street in Soho and found that they could all be linked to a particular pump, whereas other pumps and wells were disease free. He arranged for the handle to be removed from the pump to prevent its use and the disease declined. In spite of this, such was the force of the

The John Snow Inn on the site of the
infamous Broad Street Pump.
Photo: Witney Antiques

miasmatic argument that the germ theory was not fully credited until the discovery by Louis Pasteur of the bacilli of anthrax in 1879 and the discovery of the tuberculosis germ by Robert Koch, a German, in 1882. After a particularly severe outbreak of cholera in Egypt in 1893, Koch moved his laboratory there and in a few weeks had isolated the cholera germ for the first time. From this he was able to learn how chemical disinfectants and heat could kill the bacilli, and careful handling of patients could guard against passing the disease to others. By 1893 a vaccine against cholera had been developed, but even so the miasmatic theory had lingered on into the 1890s.

The Health of a Nation

Agricultural developments had led to better feeding and an improvement in health in the rural population in the previous century. The increased birthrate and survival rate provided the surplus population for the mass migration to the towns which took place with the Industrial Revolution. However, sanitation did not keep pace with either the growing towns or the industrial innovations. Overcrowding was rife. Social reformers such as Edwin Chadwick tried to draw the Government's attention to these problems. In his *Report on the Sanitary Condition of the Labouring Population* of 1842, he contrasted the expected life span of a labourer between rural Rutland, 38 years, and Manchester, 17 years. Even within Manchester the death rate per 1,000 varied from 15.8 in the middle class areas, to 35 in the most overcrowded areas.

Hygiene in Hedon

It might therefore be thought that Hedon was an unlikely place for cholera, and indeed generally the slum areas of towns were the worst affected. However, in Hedon in 1849 there were no covered sewers and no piped water supply. Effluent drained along open ditches into the streams surrounding the town. The main one followed the line of Swinegate (now George Street) and then into the Humbleton Beck along the back of Baxtergate. The town being flat and low lying, the water supply came from shallow wells and pumps. It is easy to see how, once the disease came into the town, the water supply could be quickly contaminated.

In spite of the heavy toll in 1849, no urgent steps were taken to improve the situation until 1873 when, following the threat of a new cholera epidemic, the drain was covered at the cost of 4/6 (22p) per yard. The Corporation tried to borrow £100 from the Local Government Loans Board to defray the cost and in a letter said: "the state of the open drain was such that the Urban Sanitary Authority felt bound to do the work in order that no blame should attach to the Urban Sanitary Authority should

A typical pump.

the Town again be visited by the cholera." In spite of two pleading letters the request was declined, largely on the grounds that the application should have been submitted before the work started, as is the case with grants nowadays.

The drains were continually becoming blocked, partly due to the flatness of the land and lack of sufficient fall. In 1893, the Local Government Board made, among others, the following recommendations to the Hedon Urban Sanitary District:

"The Sanitary Authority should take steps to provide a water supply for their district which is above suspicion in place of the present supplies which are subject to pollution." They "should see that all houses in the district are provided with means for getting rid of slop water without causing a nuisance. The existing sewers should be provided with a means of ventilation and flushing.Provision should be made throughout the district for the disposal of sewage in such a manner as to prevent the fouling of watercourses."

A survey of existing sewers found that the George Street sewer (a 12" brick tunnel) had over 10 inches of sediment over the greater part of its length. Indeed, when cleaned out, "its head was found with a fall of 3 to 4 inches in the wrong direction". Mr. W.H.Todd, the surveyor consulted, suggested a new drain, but, as the Sanitary Committee was considering a possible new drainage system for the Borough, it was repaired and made to do.

It would appear that the 4/6 per yard spent in 1873 was probably not enough! Similarly, the sewer at the west side of St. Augustine's Gate, which was "full of sediment and of faulty construction", was also cleaned out. However, they also replied that "disposal of sewerage [*sic*] without fouling watercourses is altogether impossible with the present system of drainage".

The Board also asked for the removal of uncovered privy middens, to which the Committee replied that "the uncovered privy middens are gradually being done away with and fixed receptacles have been considerably reduced in size. ... ... .A weekly collection of night soil has been instituted and a handbill issued stating the necessary precautions to be taken against diarrhoea." With regard to the water supply, the Committee asked the Local Government Board for "further time for consideration" and " in the meantime" issued another handbill cautioning the public to boil all water before using.

It was not until 1915 that a piped water supply came to Hedon.

HEDON
Urban Sanitary Authority.

PRECAUTIONS AGAINST

DIARRHŒA.

Every person attacked with Diarrhœa should at once secure prompt attention from a properly qualified Medical Practitioner. No case of Diarrhœa, however slight, should be neglected.

Delay in appropriate treatment often converts an easily managed ailment into a dangerous and perhaps incurable disease.

No Meat or Fish which is tainted, or Vegetables and Fruit commencing to decay, should be eaten. All Foreign Fruit should be thoroughly cooked before eaten. All Milk and all Water should be boiled before being used for cooking or drinking.

Diarrhœal Diseases, including Cholera, are **propagated mainly by filth**, the germs of disease finding their way into the human system by means of tainted air, tainted water, or tainted food. Having regard to this fact, and in view of the probable spread of diarrhœal sickness during the current season, it is desirable that the public should assist the Sanitary Authorities in their endeavours to secure the prompt removal of filth of all kinds from amidst the homes of the people.

The only Food necessary for Infants is milk, until the first teeth are cut. The old fashioned Feeding Bottles without tubes are recommended during the summer months.

One of the greatest sources of health is fresh air, hence the importance of having every room well ventilated by keeping open the doors and windows, as long as the room is not made cold thereby. Nothing which is likely to taint the air should be kept in the house. All slops and refuse should be at once removed.

Smells from Closets, Sinks, Gullies, Ashpits, etc., should be reported to the Nuisance Inspector immediately,

HENRY ROBINSON, M.B., C.M.,

MEDICAL OFFICER OF HEALTH.

HEDON, August, 1893.

Seven Fateful Weeks

August			*September*						*October*	
Sun			2	9	16	23	30			7	Sun
Mon	27		3	10	17	24		1	8	Mon
Tue	28		4	11	18	25		2	9	Tue
Wed	29		5	12	19	26		3	10	Wed
Thu	30		6	13	20	27		4	11	Thu
Fri	31		7	14	21	28		5	12	Fri
Sat		1	8	15	22	29		6		Sat

The Epidemic Reaches Hedon

In the middle of the 19th century Hedon was a rural backwater; the railway was yet to come, industry had passed it by. The inhabitants must have thought that they had escaped the problems of the big towns, including cholera, but this sense of security was shortly to be shattered.

There must have been something like panic in Hedon when it was realised that Bernard Griffith was dying of cholera. He was one of the many itinerant labourers who moved to England following the Irish famine to seek work either in agriculture, railway building, or in the heavy industry which had developed since the Industrial Revolution. Most likely he had come to Hedon to seek work with the harvest shortly to commence.

At that time cholera was raging in many of the overcrowded and insanitary cities which were expanding at a rapid rate. Where Griffith had immediately come from, we do not know, but we do know his was the first death in Hedon from the disease. He died after being ill for just 14 hours. In the Parish Register the Vicar, the Reverend James Hare Wake wrote beside his name "Died of Cholera". Before the epidemic was over he was to write this many more times.

Mary Kyme was in attendance on him and reported his death. She could not write and signed by mark. She was 53 at the time and the wife of Robert Kyme, a cartman. The family lived in Souttergate and presumably this was where Griffith died. It may perhaps be that Robert,

The carter.

the cartman brought Bernard Griffith, to Hedon, and with him the cholera!

When no more cases occurred over the next two weeks there must have been a great sense of relief, not least on the part of the two doctors of the time, Dr. Cautley, who lived in the Market Place, and Dr. Kirk of Souttergate. The sense of security was not to last. On September 15 cholera struck again: this time an unlikely place and an unlikely victim. Elizabeth Harper was a 70-year-old widow of independent means who lived in Kings Place with an elderly companion, Miss Ann Champney, also of independent means. Miss Harper was ill for 31 hours before she died. We do not know whether Miss Champney contracted the disease but we do know she survived and was later recorded as lodging with Mrs. Mary Rawson, the dressmaker, in St. Augustine's Gate.

Henry Brown's account states that "all who are taken with the disease almost invariably die". We have been unable to trace any medical records of that time for Hedon to show how many people recovered from an attack. However, experiences in other outbreaks show a 30 to 50 per cent survival rate. On this basis it seems most likely that there would be around another 30 people ill with cholera and requiring attention in addition to those who died. In most cases the cause of death is recorded as having been "certified", implying that they had been seen by a doctor, but not in all, and it is likely that many of the people who could not afford to pay a doctor's fee cared for each other, using quack remedies.

By September 16 the illness was gathering momentum. Now, not just single cases were appearing but often several in one household. Mary Jane Sleight, a child of four, died, followed two days later by her young mother. Thomas Nelthorp, a shoemaker who lived in Magdalen Gate, was a victim and also his daughter, Ann.

Jane Birk's death was the only one not mentioned in the Parish Register. Her family lived in Paull where her father, Thomas, was in business as a wheelwright. She died in Hedon, where she was most probably in service. Jane became ill on Saturday 15 September. That night her father must have been sent for, as, according to the death

The wheelwright.

certificate, he was with her when she died and he registered her death. One can imagine the panic and dread when the messenger arrived and the haste to get to her as quickly as possible. She had been ill only 16 hours when she died on the 16th. She was one of six people who died from cholera in Hedon on that day.

Objections must have been encountered to removing her body to Paull from Hedon when Paull was free of the disease. What the residents thought and said about it can easily be guessed. However, her father had his way and she was buried in the family plot in Paull churchyard. Even for those times, the Birks were an unfortunate family. She is buried in a grave with three brothers who died in infancy and three older married sisters, all of whom predeceased their mother and father.

The disease was now spreading rapidly, and in five houses in Burgess Row alone eight deaths occurred. John Batty, a wheelwright and former Parish Clerk, and his grown-up son and daughter all succumbed within two days and were buried in the family grave. Their deaths were recorded on their tombstone which can still be seen at the east side of the churchyard. Next door William Burn, the Sexton, died at a time when his services were in most demand and, next door but one, the Rawsons, husband and wife, soon followed. The Ruddiforth family must have wondered if their time had come, but, by some quirk of fate, their house escaped the disease, leaving it to pass on and claim Daniel Batty and Mary Dunn in the next two houses.

Removal and disposal of the bodies became a major problem. The National School, which stood near where the telephone exchange in Ketwell Lane now is, was taken over for use as a mortuary, and a House of Refuge was provided. Whereas the first burials were taking place one at a time with all the formalities, now it became impossible. A truck was employed to collect the bodies and take them to the school. From there they were taken for burial with little or no ceremony, mourners or followers. The Vicar entered the deaths in the Parish Register, now just identified with a "C" in the margin as though he hardly dare write the word "Cholera" any more. Services were held every night to pray for deliverance. Rev. J.S.Jones assisted the Rev. J.H.Wake, and his signature is to be found on one of the burial entries.

In the North Transept is to be found the tombstone of Caroline Askham. She was the 35-year-old wife of Thomas, a well-to-do resident of Hedon, who lived in Souttergate. She left five children motherless, a three-year-old son and four daughters, one of whom was also called Caroline. In the 1851 Census, Thomas was shown as a corn merchant. He had remarried and was living in Sheriff Highway with his new wife and family.

The death of Caroline Askham was the second to occur in Souttergate but was soon followed by others as the disease spread. Thomas Kyme, the son of Robert and Mary, who had attended Bernard Griffith, succumbed next. He was 29-years-old and described on his death certificate as a labourer. His father was present at his death. A day later it was the turn of the butcher's family, the Barons — or Baring as it is spelt in the Parish Register.Thomas Baron, his four-year-old daughter, Elizabeth, and 10-year-old son, William, died in quick succession. Thomas's widow, Frances, became a nurse with a family in St. Augustine's Gate when her remaining three children were old enough to work for themselves.

Annette Robinson had named her child Norman, an unusual name for a child in Hedon in 1849. He was one-year eight-months-old and his mother 20 when they both died on October 7.Their tombstone is in the path on the south side of the churchyard.

The Shakespeare pub in Baxtergate was still known as the Sir Charles Saunders·in 1849.The family living next door to it were a farmworker named John Elliott, his wife and their four children . Over the course of five days both parents and the youngest child had succumbed, leaving three orphaned children. There is no record of what happened to them, but their mother Jane had been born in Scotland so perhaps they were taken there by relatives to be brought up.

John Cock, the schoolmaster, escaped the illness and left Hedon shortly afterwards when the National School, with all its terrible associations, was demolished.

Bird Row was a block of four houses at the end of George Street. It

Map showing the sites of some of the pumps in Hedon.

Pumps marked P
Burgess Row is marked no 151
Swine Lane is now George Street
Note the Humbleton Beck, lower right side

13

seems strange that the houses at either end were both affected and the two middle ones were not. In the house at one end nine-year-old Sarah Ellerington died on September 17; three days later Mrs Ellen Reed (or Reid), who lived in the house at the other end, also died. The illness then returned to the Ellerington household and on the 24th Sarah's mother died, followed two days later by her father. Ellen Reed's widower, an agricultural labourer, was left with three children, two boys aged seven and five and a daughter, Sarah aged two. Shortly after, he remarried Mary Shannon, a widow, who had a son aged 12 by a previous marriage.

There were several Irish people living in Hedon in 1849. One of these was Bridget Grady. At the height of the cholera epidemic she gave birth to a daughter. She herself caught the disease and died on September 25 after being ill for only 12 hours, three days before her baby was baptised. The entry in the Parish Register describes her as an unmarried "Irish labouring woman" and gives no name for the father of the child. However, her death certificate shows her as the wife of Michael Grady, a labourer. She was 32-years-old. Her baby was named after her.

There were nine shoemakers working in Hedon in 1849, four of whom lived in St. Augustine's Gate. One of these was Robert Wilson. He and his wife, Ann, had two daughters, Harriet and Mary, both straw-bonnet makers. At the age of 15 Ann married a ships' rigger and left the Town. Both her parents perished in the epidemic and were buried in St. Augustine's Churchyard. We later hear of Mary and her children returning to Hedon to visit Harriet and the grave.

Robert Sergeant, a butcher in the Market Place, was a 43-year-old bachelor. He employed a living-in servant, Maria Spink. Maria gave her age as 20 in the 1841 census, which would have made her between 28 and 32 in 1849, as in the 1841 census ages were shown to the nearest five. In actual fact she was 37 — she had used the age-old women's prerogative of taking off a few years! Her secret was revealed when she died from cholera and her parents put up a gravestone, giving her age for all to see! Soon afterwards Sergeant employed another unmarried housekeeper, 38-year-old Elizabeth Wrias, who worked for him for many years.

Henry Brown was very accurate in the records he kept about the cholera victims. Research has found only one omission, John Jackson Todd, a baby of a year old. He was the youngest child of Abraham Todd, a bricklayer, and his wife Charlotte. They lived in George Street. John died on 28 September and his death somehow managed to be overlooked by Henry Brown, who had been so meticulous in the details he had collected.

The last victim of the disease was Elizabeth Wilson who died on 12 October. The remaining residents of Hedon must have held their breath before heaving a collective sigh of relief when they realised their ordeal was over.

General Observations

In the vestry book Henry Brown gave the number of deaths from cholera as 48, but in his list he includes "Annette Robinson and child" which he seems to have counted as only one. He never mentioned another infant, John Jackson Todd, which brings the total number of deaths up to 50.

In August 1849 Hedon had an estimated 1,000 inhabitants. In a period of less than seven weeks 50 of them, or one in 20, had died of cholera. In relation to the population, the death rate was twice as bad as in Hull, where one in 43 died during the same epidemic. The number of deaths in Hedon for a full year would normally be only 20–25.

A quarter of the population at that time — 246 — consisted of infants and children under the age of ten. There were ten deaths in this age group. At the other end of the scale, there were only 25 people in their seventies and, of these, four died, or one out of every six. Proportionally this was the worst affected section of the population as was probably only to be expected.

The crisis in Hedon occurred during the three days of Sept 25-27 when 18 people died, six on each of the three days. Almost half the deaths occurred within 12 hours of the first symptoms and only seven were after 24 hours.

Of the known addresses, only two deaths occurred in St. Augustine's Gate, one in Ivy Lane and one in Havenside. The majority of the deaths occurred in Souttergate, George Street and its associated yards, Back

Street and Burgess Row (both now Baxtergate). This no doubt reflects the sources of pollution. The open sewer ran along George Street and into the Humbleton Beck at the back of Baxtergate. The following table shows the effect on the population by age groups. Note how, apart from the very young, the percentage of deaths rises with age.

Deaths in Relation to Age

Age Group	Population	Deaths	% age of group
0 up to 10	246	10	4.06%
10 up to 20	184	3	1.63%
20 up to 30	173	8	4.62%
30 up to 40	137	8	5.84%
40 up to 50	103	5	4.85%
50 up to 60	71	6	8.45%
60 up to 70	54	5	9.25%
70 up to 80	25	4	16.00%
80 up to 90	7	1	14.23%

26 of those who died were female and 24 male, which reflects the balance in the population as a whole.

These figures have been extrapolated from the 1841 census, which showed a population of 981, plus 17 people living on boats, 998 in all.

The Churchmen

Rev. James Hare Wake

In 1849 the Rev. James Hare Wake was the Vicar of Hedon. He lived on Market Hill with his wife Caroline and their family. He had been born in Woodbridge in Suffolk and she came from Whipsnade, Bedfordshire. His conduct during the epidemic brought him great respect and admiration, and, after it was over, he was presented with a pocket Communion Service by the Corporation in recognition of his efforts. He held a church service every night, and Friday 28 September was kept as a special "day of humiliation and prayer". He spent his days conducting funerals, visiting the sick and recording deaths. The funeral bell tolled almost continuously.

Rev. Mr. Wake was interested in the fabric of the Church and in 1843 published *A Sketch of St Augustine's Church, Hedon*, describing the existence of previously hidden archways, discovered by Henry Brown and Mr. Mackereth, churchwardens. He was a great fund raiser and had no qualms about appealing to the highest in the land for contributions to the Church bazaar. He received help from Queen Adelaide and the money raised went towards the Church Restoration Fund. He was a man of bravery, ingenuity and talent and deserved the respect and affection he was given. Rev. J.H.Wake left the Hedon living in 1854.

Rev. J. S. Jones
James Samuel Jones lived in Souttergate with his wife Sarah. He was Vicar of St. Andrew's and St. Mary's Church at Paull. He was also responsible for the Chapel of Ease at Thorngumbald. He officiated at the funeral of Elizabeth Wilson, the final victim of the outbreak.

Henry Brown
Churchwarden Henry Brown lived in the Market Place and was a druggist. He was also a churchwarden and it is from his vestry book that the extract about the epidemic is taken. He had a love of elaborate language and wrote several poems on subjects about Hedon, including *John Coomber's Cross, Hedon Church Bazaar*, and a poem for the Floral Society. He was described by those who knew him as genial and convivial,interested in history, religion and poetry. He was one of the enumerators for the 1841 and the 1851 censuses and must have known most of the inhabitants of Hedon quite well.

He was married and he and his wife Ann had seven children by 1841. At the time of the cholera epidemic Brown was 43. Two years later, in the 1851 census, he was described as a widower of 46, with his 18-year-old daughter Anne acting as housekeeper and only three of the other children still at home.

During Brown's term as churchwarden restoration work was carried out on the Church and the vestry. This gave him the opportunity of removing many of the documents which were kept there, including some of the Corporation records. He later lent some of these to General Loft, the M.P. for Grimsby, who never returned them. The Loft family lost money and sold the records to Gillyat Sumner, who lived in Beverley but had interests in Hedon. Sumner also managed to get papers from the Hedon solicitor, William Watson. Then he discovered that Henry Brown had managed to acquire even more of the Corporation records and these were still in his possession. Brown received money for the papers, which, of course, he had no right to sell. Fortunately Gillyat Sumner preserved them carefully and after Sumner's death the papers were bought for Hedon Corporation.

The Medical Men

Dr. Henry Cautley

Dr. Henry Cautley lived in Souttergate at what is now the Paddock with his wife Mary Ann née Clapham, born in Burton Pidsea, and their children. He was a Member (later Fellow) of the Royal College of Surgeons and a Licensed Apothecary. At the time of the cholera outbreak he was 51 and his wife 47. He was the son of the Rev. John Cautley and was born at Dunnington Rectory, near York. His father died young, Henry was only six, and he was probably brought up by his grandfather, also Rev. John Cautley who was the rector of Upper Helmsley. Both his father and grandfather are buried in Dunnington churchyard.

Following the outbreak he became interested in the running of the Town and in 1860 stood as a candidate for the party trying to reform the Council. He gained only 23 votes and was defeated, but, nothing daunted, he stood again and this time was elected.

He died in 1874 at the age of 76 and his memorial can be seen near the north-east corner in St. Augustine's Church.

Dr. William Kirk

Dr. William Kirk, also a Member of the Royal College of Surgeons and a Licensed Apothecary, was 41 years of age at the time of the cholera. His birthplace was Kimberworth, between Sheffield and Rotherham. He married a local Hedon girl, Frances, also 41 at the time of the epidemic, and they lived with their five children at Kirk House in the Market Place. He was family doctor to the Constable family of Burton Constable Hall, from whom he received several gifts. He employed two female servants, and a groom with the unlikely name of Cornelius Harker to look after the pony and trap which he used for his visits round the district.

Like his fellow doctor, Henry Cautley, William Kirk was interested in the running of the Town. He also belonged to the group of reformers and stood for election in November 1860 with several like-minded candidates. They were all defeated but at his next attempt he won a seat. He progressed to be elected Mayor of Hedon in 1870; the first Mayor of the Borough who was not also a Freeman. Such was the respect for him that he was to fill this office five times.

He died in 1891 at the age of 83 and is buried in the churchyard near the west door of St. Augustine's.

Mr. Arden, the House Visitor

During the Hull cholera outbreak a system of house visitation was set up. When the cholera broke out this was extended to Hedon and Mr. Arden was appointed to Hedon as the House Visitor. His official duties were as follows:

"He should visit every house in his district once a day at least, and, in cases of sudden attacks in confined localities, at much shorter intervals, as may be necessary. He should inform the people of the object of his visits on going round the first time; and, if possible, he should on this occasion see every person in the house and converse with them, in order that they may be able to render every information and assistance to the Visitor on his subsequent visits. The Visitor should impress on people the necessity of attending to the earliest symptom of derangement of the bowels and direct them specially to apply to the nearest dispensary or to the District Medical Officer if taken ill during the interval between his visits.

"The Visitor should carry with him suitable medicines to administer to all persons suffering from cholera or from premonitory symptoms, and exhibit them on the spot, where required. He should also give such information or caution as may appear requisite in regard to the cleanliness of persons or houses, the danger of overcrowding, the necessity for ventilation, the evils of drinking habits and other similar matters."

Any cases he found he was to treat until further assistance arrived.Each day he had to make a return to the doctor in charge of the scheme and, when a case had occurred and was resolved, he had to make sure the house was thoroughly cleansed and limewashed

It was obviously a very hard and dangerous job and praise was given to him by " an Inhabitant of Hedon", who wrote to the *Hull Advertiser* on 28 September 1849: "The diminution is no doubt attributable to the house to house visitations by Mr. Arden on the same principle as that in Hull."

Clearly Mr. Arden took his Herculean task seriously and performed it well.

Henry Brown, Druggist

See the previous section on the Church.

James Soutter, Druggist

James Soutter, born 1793, was the son of Alderman John Soutter. His father set him up as a druggist and grocer in a shop in St. Augustine's Gate, near the corner of George Street, an area which the Soutter family seem to have made their own. In 1849 James was 56-years-old and still unmarried, living with his younger brother, John. John was a blacksmith and he and his wife, Mary Ann, had eight children. James took John's third son, James Stewart, who was 17 at the time of the epidemic, into the business with him.

James was a Freeman of Hedon and a member of the old reactionary faction. He was Mayor five times and was the last Freeman to be Mayor before the Borough Improvement Act opened the way for the reformers.James died in 1872 aged 79 and is buried in St. Augustine's Church.

The Public Officials

Arthur Iveson — The Coroner

At the time of the cholera outbreak the Coroner was Arthur Iveson, a member of the well-known Hedon family about whom much has been written elsewhere. He was then an attorney, 42-years-old and lived in Fletchergate in the New Hall. He and his wife, Mary, had five children, all of whose names began with "A": Alice, Arthur, Albert, Albina and Ada.

On the death of his uncle, James Iveson, in 1850, Arthur acquired the posts of Town Clerk and Clerk to the County Court. He was also an Alderman. Together with the Freemen he ran Hedon and it was against the rule of this oligarchy that the reform movement in which the doctors played a prominent part was directed. He died in 1881 and was buried in St. Augustine's churchyard.

John Day — The Registrar

John Day was a tallow chandler, then aged 33. He and his wife, Elizabeth, lived in the Market Place. He was interested in the running of the Town and held the office of Registrar during the cholera epidemic. Some of the death certificates he wrote at the time were very sparse in detail, often omitting the description and address of the deceased and the informant, and merely writing "Hedon".

Patent Remedies

As is usual at a time of crisis there were many entrepreneurs ready to take advantage of the public's credibility. Some weird and wonderful remedies were advertised with amazing claims for their efficacy. If they had all worked, the epidemic would have ended in hours! Older remedies, such as a regular intake of brandy, or burning tar barrels to clear the air of infection, were still used but the advertisements for "miracle cures" must have had a strong attraction.

This is the prescription for Dr. Gibbs' remedy, for which it was claimed he was made a Knight of St. Vladimir in recognition of his valuable services in St. Petersburg:-

> 2 drachms   Aromatic Confection
> 7 ounces   Camphor Mixture or Julen
> 40 drops or minims of Tincture of Opium
> 2 drachms   Compound Spirit of Ammonia or Sal Volatile
> ½ ounce   Tincture of Ginger.

Dose: 2 to 3 tablespoonfuls to be taken 2 or 3 times a day — or as required.

The effect of such a concoction must have been quite remarkable.

"*The only genuine.*"

Another cure, published in the *Hull Advertiser* on July 7 1849 was for: Reinhardt's Anti-Cholera Mixture — "the only genuine". J. G. Reinhardt was a chemist and druggist in the Market Place, Hull. He sold his remedy in two sizes, bottles priced 1s.0d or 2s.6d (five or 12 pence) each, "with full directions". He mentions in the same advertisement that he is also the agent for Biggs Sheepdipping Composition. One wonders whether there was very much difference between the two.

Doctors prescribed their own favourite remedies, including calomel, rhubarb, castor oil, laudanum and chalk. Acetate of lead, nitrate of silver, opium, ammonia and citrate of potash were all used. Sometimes hot air baths were recommended, and also the use of mustard plasters. Mustard seemed to be a favourite medicine and "Kingston Mustard", manufactured in "a new and scientific manner" by Simpson Hall & Co of Hull, was sold in jars of 1lb, 1/2lb and 1/4lb.

Dr. Fleischman advertised his Cholera Drops, reputed to have been administered to 150,000 people in Vienna, and Sir William Burnett's Patent Disinfecting Fluid — "sealed with a cork" — was highly recommended. There was even a money-back offer from one Thomas Sleighty who offered to pay £5 to the Infirmary for anyone taking his Herbal Bowel Mixture and not recovering! Some of these "cures" were more likely to kill, but their inventors probably did not stay around long enough to face any repercussions.

There were many suggestions for "Clearing the Air"; no doubt from people believing in the miasma theory. A correspondent to the *Hull Advertiser* wrote that "as no thunderstorms seemed imminent", all the large guns of the Garrison should be fired together, thus achieving the desired effect.

Another idea was for each household to keep a bucket of chloride of lime and a large stick by the door. It was to be stirred vigorously upon entering and leaving the house in order that the fumes released could penetrate the building and purify it. If the inhabitants were saved from the cholera they were probably asphyxiated.

There was a popular street song sung to the tune of *The Campbells are Coming* — "The cholera's coming, oh dear, oh dear".

It did come and the medical knowledge of the day was powerless against it.

Cholera Today

During the 19th century there were six waves of cholera spreading out from India to the Middle East, Europe and the U.S.A. By the early 20th century, good sanitation, pure water and medical advances had defeated the disease in the developed countries and it was gradually driven back to its heartland in southern Asia. The disease remained quiescent until 1961 when a major outbreak occurred in the Phillipines. This was caused by a different strain of the bacteria which had caused the epidemics of the 19th century. Since then the disease has made something of a come-back, spreading over Africa and reaching parts of the world not prevously affected.

In 1990, a grain boat from the East returned to port in Peru due to an outbreak of cholera. The crew came ashore and stayed a few days for treatment and to recover. None of the crew died. Cholera cases began to appear along the coast and rapidly spread inland, reaching the headwaters of the Amazon. By 1992 the number of notified cases in Peru was 200,000. The disease continued on its way, helped by the tendency of the population along the Amazon to use the river and its tributaries for all purposes and has now reached the sea. The disease is also spreading to the north across central America.

The modern treatment for cholera is rehydration, to replace the rapid loss of bodily fluids and salts, and treatment with tetracycline or similar drugs to kill the bacteria and reduce the period of diarrhoea. The amount of rehydration required is massive as patients can lose 20% of their body weight in a day. The rehydration can be given orally and can be made by adding five grams of salt and 20 grams of glucose, or 40 grams of sucrose (sugar) to one litre of water, although medical authorities would use a slightly more sophisticated version of this solution and in severe cases administer the solution intravenously.

Historically, vaccines have not been wholly effective, giving only 90% protection with the effect lasting for only a short period, but in recent years methods of enhancing the effect have resulted in great improvements.

The main weapon against cholera is still that put forward by Dr.John Snow* 150 years ago — a pure water supply and an efficient system for the disposal of sewage. In the developed world we must ensure the systems for achieving this are kept in good order. We are seeing in Bosnia the infrastructure being destroyed by war. Let us hope the warring factions make peace and repair the damage before cholera again comes back to Europe.

For the Third World the answer still lies in the future. What good is it telling people to boil water if they cannot afford the fuel to do so? It must be the responsibility of govern-ments to educate and provide the necessary facilities, and the developed world must play its part in helping them. We are one world and disease recognises no boundaries.

The Red Granite kerbstone marks the site of the historic BROAD STREET PUMP associated with Dr. John Snow's discovery in 1854 that Cholera is conveyed by water

* An interesting connection between John Snow and Hedon. Adjacent to the Broad Street Pump and affected by its malign influence were Pulteney Court, Great Pulteney Street and Little Pulteney Street; on the fringe of John Snow's map lie Heddon Court and Heddon Street — all named in honour of Hedon's 18th century M.P. William Pulteney.

EXTRACT from the Minutes of the Hedon Parish Church Vestry Book written by Mr Henry Brown, Churchwarden, and dated Hedon, Sept.1849

"The people are panic stricken, the inhabitants of ancient Hedon are siezed with fearful amazement, the stoutest hearts tremble, The LORD has a controversy with the people and is now visiting for sin. The Cholera has come amongst us and is now carrying off its victims so numerous; and at a rate so fearfully rapid, that a sort of stupor appears to have fastened upon the place and all, aye all, are at their wits ends. Groups assemble in the streets and Cholera and death are the only things talked about. The constant appearance of Doctors and Nurses and busy Parochial Officials, and Undertakers, and Sanitary Agents, and Corpses and Coffins; with the continuous sound of the Funeral Bell, make it absolutely a place of tears, of sighs, and of groans in which it is misery to dwell.

"All who are taken with the disease almost invariably die and that after an illness of very few hours; and disobedience to medical treatment appears a remarkable characteristic of this dreadful scourge. At first the dead were permitted to remain at their homes and after an interval of few hours were interred. Now the deaths are so frequent and follow each other with such awful rapidity, sometimes seven or eight in one day, that a truck is now employed for their removal to the National School which has been converted into a Dead House. From thence they are borne to the grave upon a Bier by two or four men, and often trailed there on the same truck, without the usual attendance of mourners and in most instances without the attendance of a single follower. The occupants of some houses have been entirely cut off, and their habitations left tenantless, and many, very many, are made desolate. Services are being held nightly in the Church and Friday, the 28th inst., has been kept as a day of humiliation and prayer; and unless the Lord stays the plague who may be spared.
....
.... (blank left in original)
"Blessed be the LORD he has heard and answered prayer; the Cholera has departed from our town, and the Parish can again present a "clean bill of health". Yes the Cholera has departed after having taken about one in eighteen of the whole population and that in the short space of eighteen or twenty days! Yes the Cholera has departed, and I, sinful I, am left to make this record!! In return may I renew my covenant afresh with Thee and let the bond of the covenant be everlasting Love.

"And now after the Judgements of the Lord have been so fearfully abroad, will the people, will the inhabitants of Hedon learn righteousness? There appears to be a deep impression made upon many, may it be lasting, may those who have been brought safely through this time of decease *(sic)*, of pestilence and death, feel their additional responsibility to GOD; may they turn unto Him with full purpose of heart; may they make their calling and election sure; may the penman of this imperfect description of the late troublous time be of the number so we that all at the time of CHRIST's coming to judge quick and dead may be found an acceptance *(sic)* people in His sight. 'They that sow in tears shall reap in joy. He that goeth forth and weepeth bearing precious seed, shall doubtless come again with rejoicing bringing his sheaves with him.'

"The numbers who died from Cholera were 48, viz:

August 27.	Bernard Griffith in 14 hours
Sept 15.	Eliz. Harper. 31
16.	Mary Jane Sleight. 5
	Thos. Nelthorp. 24
17.	Jane Birks.
16	Caroline Askham. 9
	Sarah Ellerington. 17
	Mary McHale. 36
	Daniel Batty. 10
18.	Jane Sleight. 7
17.	Wm. Burn. 5
19.	Susan Brown 24
20.	Ellen Reid. 2½ days
	Eliz. Hodgson. 2 days 3hrs
21.	Martin Bell. 10 hours
	Mary Dunn. 3 days 12hrs
	Ann Nelthorp. 16 hours
24.	Ann Ellerington. 9
25.	John Burn. 9
	Jane Collingwood. 12
	Bridget Grady. 12
	Robert Elliott. 23
	Richard Wright. 11
	Thos. Kyme. 26
	Hannah Burn 8
	Wm Baron 8
	Eliz. Baron. 6
	Thomas Bell. 19
	Jonathan Ellerington. 12
	Agnes Rawson. 14
27.	Jane Elliott, 13
	Patrick Kelly. 3 Days
	John Batty. 14 Hours

	Joseph Batty. 8
	Ann Wilson. 8
	Rachel Cross. 8
28.	Robt. Wilson. 18
	Martha Batty. 16
30.	Wm.Smith. not recorded
	John Elliott. 12 hours
	Thos. Baron. 10
Oct. 1.	Maria Spink. 10
2.	Matthew Burn. 20
	George Robinson. 12
3.	Susan Bell. 18
6.	Francis Rawson. 33
7.	Annette Robinson & child. 18
12.	Eliz Wilson. 8½

"Many are the opinions and theories put forth as being the cause of this late calamitous visitation. Some will have it that the air is charged with a morbific poison; some blame the Rivers and talk of Miasmata. Others there are who affirm that they have espied in the waters of springs and wells Animalculae and Fungi. Others again are denouncing Gutters and Sewers, and Ash Heaps and Dunghills and the like; all of which have been in existence ever since mankind have congregated together in towns and cities.

"For myself I believe all the foregoing notions are erroneous. We have ever had and still have the same Rivers; we have ever drank and still drink of the same waters; we have ever had, but we now have not half so many dirty Gutters, foul Sewers and the like as formerly — and yet we have not now, or ever had before the Cholera. Nor can it be the air or why should Marfleet, and Paull and Thorn and Burstwick and Barton with other neighbouring villages not have been visited?

"I believe an all merciful Providence has not made us with frames so defective, as to endanger our lives by coming in contact with the smells and annoyances which are common and necessarily appendant to our fallen nature. I believe He who is Infinite, with whom past present and future are the same, He who maketh the clouds His chariot and walketh upon the wings of the wind, He with whom are the issues of life and death. I believe that He has thousands of natural agents that are far removed from human knowledge, and that some of those have been used in working out the purposes of GOD I readily admit; but for anyone to say that, is altogether speculative. I know that cleanliness brings comfort, and that therefore good sewerage and good drainage are not only necessary but commendable but after all, this is not the cause of, will never prevent or cure the Cholera.

'I came to the place of my birth, and cried "The friends of my youth, where are they?" An echo replied "Where are they?" '

Further Extract dated Dec. 15th. 1849.
"Public Day of Prayer and Thanksgiving to Almighty God for His goodness vouchsafed to the Kingdom in removing the Cholera. Services held in the Church morning and evening and the day kept holy as the Sabbath."

Appendix ii

Where tombstones may be seen

St Augustine's Church, Hedon.

Inside
North-east corner of
Choir —   Dr. Henry Cautley
North Transept —   Caroline Askham   *

Churchyard
Path of tombstones on east side

John Batty	)	*
Joseph Batty	)	*
Martha Batty	)	*
Susan Brown		*
Maria Spink		*

Path of tombstones on south side

Matthew Burn		*
Thomas Kyme		*
Annette Robinson	)	*
[Annetta in Parish Register]	)	
Norman Robinson	)	*
Ann Wilson	)	*
Robert Wilson	)	*

West end (near door)
     Dr. William Kirk
     Arthur Iveson
     James Soutter

St. Andrew's and St. Mary's Church, Paull

South side of churchyard
     Jane Birks   *
     (with six brothers and sisters)
     (mother and father adjacent)

*denotes cholera victim
) Names of those in the same grave are bracketed together

Alphabetical list of those   who died

Name	Forename	Name	Forename
Askham	Caroline	Elliott	Robert
Baron (Baring)	Eliz	Grady	Bridget
Baron (Baring)	Thomas	Griffith	Bernard
Baron (Baring)	William	Harper	Eliz
Batty	Daniel	Hodgson	Eliz
Batty	John	Kelly	Patrick
Batty	Joseph	Kyme	Thomas
Batty	Martha	McHale	Mary
Bell	Martin	Nelthorp	Ann
Bell	Susannah	Nelthorp	Thomas
Bell	Thomas	Rawson	Agnes
Birks	Jane	Rawson	Francis
Brown	Susan	Reid (Read or	
Burn	Hannah	Reed)	Ellen
Burn	John	Robinson	Annette (Annetta)
Burn	Matthew	Robinson	George
Burn	Wm	Robinson	Norman
Collingwood	Jane	Sleight	Jane
Cross	Rachel	Sleight	Mary Jane
Dunn	Mary	Smith	Wm
Ellerington	Ann	Spink	Maria
Ellerington	Jonathan	Todd	John Jackson
Ellerington	Sarah	Wilson	Ann
Elliott	Jane	Wilson	Eliz
Elliott	John	Wilson	Robt
		Wright	Richard

Is your surname amongst those above?

Have you any historical information regarding your forebears?

Do you wish to know more?

If so please write to Margaret and Bob Cochrane c/o Highgate Publications, 24 Wylies Road, Beverley HU17 7AP.